bubonic plague, fire consumed much of London, armies fought throughout the kingdom, England became a republic and then a monarchy once more, and the last Stuart king was forced into exile, leaving his two daughters to rule successively in his place.

Many ordinary people rose to great prominence; those such as Guy Fawkes, Oliver Cromwell, Samuel Pepys, Isaac Newton, Nell Gwynne and Christopher Wren remain famous to this day. Collectively, they made 17th-century and early 18th-century England a place of decisive action and lasting achievement.

King Charles II, surrounded by his courtiers, strides across Horse Guard's Parade in 17th-century London. The energetic king was very fond of walking — normally at a brisk pace, much to the alarm of his less fit followers.

The Age of the Stuarts

Plague delayed the arrival of James I into London for his coronation and he was not crowned until 1604, the year after he became king. James wished to unite both his kingdoms but this was firmly resisted by the English parliament.

Aturbulent undercurrent of religious unrest ran throughout virtually the entire Stuart era, causing James I to narrowly escape assassination, Charles I to lose his head and James II to forfeit his crown. Religious conflict helped to cause a bloody civil war and led to a republic for the only time in the nation's history. Religious extremism dominated, as the Puritans – hardline Nonconformists – clashed with the established Church, and traditional Roman Catholics were discriminated against and marginalised.

Successive Stuart kings struggled to cope with this unhappy state of affairs and nearly all failed. Four Stuart kings created suspicion by marrying Roman Catholic wives. When James II fathered a Roman Catholic son, it cost him the kingdom. The situation was saved by James II's two Protestant daughters – Mary and Anne. Mary's husband, the Dutch ruler William of Orange, was invited to become king, largely because he was a Protestant. In 1701 the Act of Settlement laid down that no Roman Catholic could thereafter become monarch.

New reigns usually begin with optimism so, when James I came to power, expectations ran high. Catholics hoped for greater tolerance; Puritans expected more understanding from a king from Presbyterian Scotland; Parliament anticipated a far more important role than had been experienced under the Tudors. All were massively disappointed, causing religious and political discord and creating a long, bitter conflict between monarch and Parliament that was to end in civil war. By the end of the century, however, the balance of power had dramatically shifted. The authority of Queen Anne was markedly less than that enjoyed by Queen Elizabeth I

The ships at anchor in the Medway fly the Union Jack, which was created after James I became king of both England and Scotland. It combined the flags of both nations and is nicknamed a 'jack' because it flew on the jackstaff of naval warships.

just a hundred years earlier. Parliament finally gained an effective voice, and England and Scotland moved closer together politically, until in 1707 they were united by the Act of Union and became one country, Great Britain.

Monumental change was also taking place in continental Europe. Spain, England's erstwhile arch-enemy during Elizabethan times, was in decline, and France was very much in the ascendancy, while the newly created republic of Holland was both aggressive and acquisitive. Having hovered on the edge of the international stage for much of the 17th century, Britain was ultimately to emerge as an extremely powerful commercial and trading nation, with an expanding overseas empire that included several American colonies.

Daniel Mytens' picture, now in the Royal Collection, depicts King Charles I together with his French-born wife, Queen Henrietta Maria. She was to prove a staunch supporter of the king during the subsequent Civil War.

John Rose, the king's gardener, presents Charles II with the first pineapple grown in England. Many exotic new species were imported during the Stuart era, primarily by John Tradescant when he was royal gardener — 'keeper of His Majesty's gardens, vines and silkworms'.

The Tower of London continued to be a prison and a place of execution for prominent people. Amongst those beheaded there during the Stuart era were Sir Walter Raleigh, Archbishop Laud, the Dukes of Argyll and Monmouth, and the Earl of Strafford.

Gunpowder, Treason and Plot

Religious extremism emerged early in the reign of James I. On Sunday 20 May 1604, five fanatical Roman Catholics met secretly at the Duck & Drake, a London inn, to hear their leader, Robert Catesby, make a sensational proposal – blow up King James I along with his entire Parliament. A member of the group was to become one of the most notorious figures in English history – his name was Guy Fawkes.

The Gunpowder Plot, as it is known today, was a spectacular plan, even by modern terrorist standards, yet these conspirators were not a highly trained assassination squad, but an idealistic bunch of amateurs who were angered by the king's failure to tolerate their religion. The plot was doomed from the start.

Catesby and two fellow conspirators were already under surveillance by

After the discovery of the Gunpowder Plot and the arrest of the conspirators, King James I gave an emotional speech to the assembled members of the Houses of Parliament. The plotters are shown in the cellars underneath.

A melodramatic contemporary print portrays Guy Fawkes and his fellow conspirators wearing tall hats and swirling cloaks. To this day the cellars of the House of Lords are ceremoniously searched prior to the State Opening of Parliament.

The iron lantern carried by Guy Fawkes at the time of his arrest can now be seen in the Ashmolean Museum, Oxford, to which it was presented by Robert Heywood, the son of one of the Justices of the Peace who apprehended Guy Fawkes.

government secret agents, following their part in the Earl of Essex's abortive rising of 1601, and haphazard recruitment of additional plotters further compromised secrecy. The Powder Treason, as it was then called, quickly came to the attention of the cunning and unscrupulous Sir Robert Cecil, James' Chief Minister, who immediately seized the opportunity to further discredit Roman Catholics.

An anonymous letter to Lord Monteagle, a Roman Catholic peer and relative of one of the conspirators, warned him not to attend the opening of Parliament and was immediately shown to Cecil. At the same time, one of the plotters turned Government informer. Early on the morning of 5 November 1605, Guy Fawkes was apprehended in a vault below the House of Lords with 36 barrels of gunpowder. The rest of the plotters fled to the country, but were either killed resisting arrest or captured and imprisoned in the Tower of London along with the luckless Fawkes. Subsequently all were tortured, tried, then hanged, drawn and quartered. The gunpowder subsequently proved to be decayed and would never have exploded. Monteagle was awarded a government pension and Cecil was created Earl of Salisbury. Persecution of Roman Catholics increased for many years and even now on 5 November effigies of Guy Fawkes burn on bonfires throughout the country.

The shaky nature of Guy Fawkes' signature on a document confessing to his part in the Gunpowder Plot is the result of torture while confined in the Tower of London.

The Pilgrim Fathers

In the autumn of 1620 the Pilgrim Fathers set sail from Plymouth for the New World in order to acquire more freedom to practise their beliefs. The voyage was a supreme example of Puritan faith and fortitude. Having crossed 2,000 miles of storm-tossed Atlantic Ocean, they landed on a bleak, inhospitable shore, behind which lay thick forest inhabited by native 'Indians', rumoured to flay their captives' bodies with fish shells before cutting off pieces to cook in front of their victims. 'All great and honourable actions are accompanied with great difficulties, and must be both enterprised and overcome with answerable courages. The dangers are great but not desperate, the difficulties many but not invincible,' one of their leaders, William Bradford, reassured any doubters after they landed. Bradford later became governor of the new colony.

The steps on the Barbican in Plymouth from where the Pilgrim Fathers departed is marked today by a plaque and the flags of Britain and the United States. Nearby is Island House, where the Pilgrims gathered prior to sailing, and the museum, Mayflower Plymouth, where their achievements are displayed.

Jean Leon Jerome Ferris' picture portrays the Pilgrim Fathers sharing the first Thanksgiving with the 'Indians' who helped them survive their first year on the new continent.

Most of the group had originally come from Yorkshire and Nottinghamshire, where they had become disenchanted with existing religious practices. After an unsatisfactory attempt to settle in Holland they petitioned King James I for permission to go to Virginia. When the sceptical king asked how they proposed to live, they replied 'by fishing'. 'So God have my soul,' declared a delighted James, ''tis an honest trade! 'Twas the Apostles' own calling.'

Thus the intrepid group of Puritans joined 66 West Country adventurers to set sail in the *Mayflower*, a vessel of only 180 tons. They landed in Cape Cod Bay, north of Virginia, amidst a harsh, unforgiving winter. Some had perished on the voyage, others succumbed to disease, starvation or sheer exhaustion. Yet faith, hard work and assistance surprisingly given to them by the supposedly hostile 'Indians' ensured that enough survived to found the new town of Plymouth, in modern-day Massachusetts. Their first successful harvest the following year was marked by Thanksgiving, an occasion still celebrated in the United States today.

Several attempts had been made to set up a colony in North America before the Pilgrim Fathers' successful voyage. This Indian settlement in North Carolina was painted by John White in 1587. Native Americans showed the settlers which crops to plant and gave them food and seeds.

*The Pilgrim Fathers landed in New England in the winter of 1620. First ashore was John Alder, a cooper. In the background is the **Mayflower** which had carried the settlers across the Atlantic Ocean. By spring, half of them had perished.*

7

The Civil War

A relentless struggle, particularly over money and religion, between the autocratic King Charles I and hardline members of Parliament determined to achieve greater power, began soon after Charles inherited the throne in 1625. The rebels distrusted the Chief Minister, Buckingham, resented unsanctioned taxes and were suspicious of the king's High Church attitudes. Charles managed to rule without calling a parliament for 11 years. Finally, his clumsy attempt to arrest five MPs, including his chief critics, Pym and Hampden, led to outright war in 1642.

A contemporary cartoon displays the animosity between the opposing sides during the Civil War. The expressions 'Cavalier' and 'Roundhead' were both terms primarily of insult. As the war progressed, the bitterness between the sides increased throughout the divided nation.

Battles were to rage from Yorkshire to Cornwall. London, the south-east and East Anglia largely supported the Parliamentarians, while most of Wales, the West Country, the north and much of the Midlands favoured the Royalists. Aristocracy and gentry featured on both sides, as did ordinary folk. Lifelong friends fought each other and families were divided.

This 19th-century picture graphically captures the dreadful carnage at the Battle of Marston Moor near York in 1644. Defeat for King Charles meant he lost the whole of northern England.

When the king raised his standard at Nottingham, the wind blew it over. Yet after this inauspicious beginning the war went well for Charles, who displayed an unexpected relish for campaigning, together with a quick grasp of tactics. Superior cavalry under the dashing Prince Rupert ensured a tentative Royalist success in 1642 at Edgehill, the first major battle. By the end of 1643, the king had won a string of victories and controlled most of the nation.

Charles failed to take London, however, and in the summer of 1644 the tide turned at Marston Moor near York, where Oliver Cromwell's cavalry shattered the king's forces in the largest and bloodiest battle of the war. Four thousand Royalist corpses littered the battlefield. 'God made them as stubble to our swords,' declared Cromwell, who, along with other commanders of the Parliamentarian New Model Army, such as Ireton and Harrison, and their psalm-singing Puritan troops, saw the war as a crusade to establish a new political and religious order amidst the towns and countryside of 17th-century England.

The following summer Charles was comprehensively defeated at Naseby by Cromwell's highly disciplined New Model Army. Although the war continued until the spring of 1646, flaring briefly again in 1648, defeat for Charles and the Royalist cause was now inevitable. His long journey to the scaffold had begun.

Prince Rupert, a nephew of Charles I, charges opposing Parliamentarian cavalry during the Battle of Edgehill in Warwickshire in October 1642. The prince was courageous but too impetuous. The indiscipline of his troops at Edgehill prevented a decisive Royalist victory.

Oliver Cromwell, as seen in 1649 by Samuel Cooper, the leading miniaturist of the day. His work can now be found in the National Portrait Gallery in London. Cromwell valued realism, exhorting one artist to paint him 'warts and all'.

'Man of Blood' – Charles I

Charles had been a sickly child, who spoke with a stutter and, like many shy people, appeared aloof and disdainful. He was a poor judge of character and was heavily influenced by the last person he spoke to. He was dominated first by Buckingham, his Chief Minister, and later by his feisty French wife, Henrietta Maria. Ultimately King Charles' inability to handle Parliament led to the turmoil of the Civil War and his own downfall.

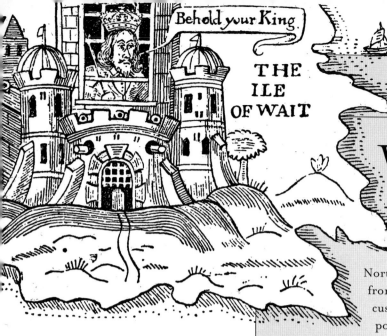

Behold your King.

THE
ILE
OF WAIT

A contemporary cartoon of Charles I imprisoned in Carisbrooke Castle on the Isle of Wight, aptly renamed here the isle of 'Wait'. Today the castle is a popular tourist attraction.

Van Dyck's brilliant triple portrait of King Charles I was painted in order to assist the Italian sculptor Bernini, who had been commissioned to sculpt the king. When Bernini saw Van Dyck's picture, he declared, 'This is a portrait of a doomed man.'

The Last Days of Charles I

When Charles I realised that the war was lost, he naively sought refuge with the Scottish army, who handed him over to Parliamentary Commissioners for £200,000. The king was taken to Holdenby House in Northamptonshire, but he was seized from here by the army and taken into custody. Charles was in a perilous position. At Hampton Court he had a series of meetings with Cromwell and Ireton. When Charles arrogantly declared, 'You cannot do without me, you will fall to ruin if I do not sustain you,' Cromwell decided that negotiations were pointless. Charles then escaped to the Isle of Wight and, whilst in Carisbrooke Castle, arranged a treaty with the Scots. They provided him with an army, which invaded England but was quickly defeated.

The king's double-dealing completed his downfall and he was brought to London to face a charge of high treason. The legality of the trial was dubious, and most leading legal figures refused to attend. Cromwell, however, was not concerned with the finer points of the law. 'I tell you, we will cut off his head with the crown upon it,' he bluntly told the Commissioners assembled to try the king in Westminster Hall, scene of many dramatic state trials.

The king sealed his fate by disdainfully refusing to acknowledge the authority of the court and answer the charges, 'eyeing his judges with unaffected scorn'. The sentence was, 'The said Charles Stuart, as tyrant, traitor, murderer and a public enemy, shall be put to death by severing his head from his body.' On a bitterly cold January afternoon in 1649, Charles was executed outside the Banqueting House at Whitehall Palace. As the axe fell, an onlooker commented, 'there was such a groan by the thousands there present as I have never heard before and desire may never hear again.'

Ernest Croft's Victorian painting shows King Charles on the scaffold immediately prior to execution, watched by a huge crowd of soldiers. As it was a bitterly cold day Charles wore two shirts to avoid shivering and so appearing frightened at the prospect of his impending death.

A contemporary print of the trial of Charles I in Westminster Hall in London. Charles faces the Parliamentary Commissioners whose chairman, William Bradshaw, fearing assassination, wore a bullet-proof hat.

Cromwell gazed down at the king's headless body laid out in Westminster Hall, after an execution which appalled the whole of Europe. 'Cruel necessity,' he is said to have declared. Parliament abolished the monarchy and the House of Lords and declared England to be a Commonwealth. The Puritans were in power.

Henry Chorley of Preston Haberdasher.

John the son of Henry. Josiah his Brother. Joseph his Brother.

Ellin the wife of Henry Chorley.

Henry his Brother.

Daniel his Brother.

Samuel his Brother.

The Chorleys were a typical Puritan family, soberly dressed in black and appropriately pious. Henry Chorley was a haberdasher from Preston in Lancashire.

An oak tree in the grounds of Boscobel House, once a 17th-century hunting lodge. The tree's famous predecessor was the one in which Charles II supposedly hid from Cromwell's troops after his defeat at the Battle of Worcester in 1651, when he unsuccessfully tried to regain the throne.

Life Under the Puritans

The brave new world of Puritan England appears to have been a worthy yet rather dull place. Rigorous attempts to eradicate all forms of vice resulted in many ale houses being closed, while gambling, together with horse racing, bear-baiting and cockfighting, were forbidden. Theatres were forcibly closed, swearing fined, and prostitutes whipped and branded. Athletics, wrestling, even dancing around the village maypole, were no longer allowed, and walking on a Sunday, except to church, was banned. Christmas festivities were frowned on by the authorities, and feast days were replaced by a monthly fast day. The sole feast day permitted was 5 November, which celebrated the discovery of the Gunpowder Plot — it is ironic that the saving of King James was commemorated by a regime that had executed his son.

Sweeping changes took place in religious practices. The Prayer Book was replaced by the Directory, introducing a shorter, more spartan form of service. Weddings were conducted by magistrates rather than priests, with no drinking or dancing after the ceremony. Baptisms and burials were equally brief. Both Anglicans and Roman Catholics kept a low profile, although Cromwell interestingly permitted the return of Jews to England after centuries of exile, convinced that they were the true guardians of the Old Testament that the Puritans so revered. It was also said that the Second Coming would take place in Puritan England and Cromwell reasoned that this prospect might be enhanced with Jews present. The Quaker movement began, supposedly named because its founder, George Fox, exhorted people 'to quake at the name of the Lord'.

Since the deaths of capable politicians, such as John Hampden and John Pym, with their sharp minds, sharp tongues, and passion for the rule of law, the Parliament of the Commonwealth lacked stature. 'An end to your prating, you are no Parliament,' Cromwell cried. In 1653 Cromwell was created Lord Protector and ruled alone until his death in 1658. His far less capable son, Richard, then became Protector, but, failing to gain respect, was nicknamed 'Tumbledown Dick'. As anarchy threatened, the mood of the nation favoured a return of the monarchy. Life had become too serious under the Puritans.

Contemporary cartoons give contrasting views of Cromwell. He is portrayed in the picture above carrying the Bible, the dove of peace flying above his head, and in the drawing below wearing the horns of the devil as he presides over his Council.

Today Oliver Cromwell's statue proudly stands outside the Houses of Parliament, whose rights and privileges, as MP, soldier and statesman, he campaigned so hard to protect.

OLIVER CROMWELL 1599 1658

Some have greatness thrust upon them ... – Cromwell

Oliver Cromwell was an obscure, middle-aged country squire who became a great military commander and reluctant head of State. In war, Cromwell never lost a battle, convinced that he was 'the sword of God'. He was loved and admired by his followers, but feared and hated by his opponents. In 1657 Parliament offered to crown him king, but he refused.

'... the way strewn with flowers, the bells ringing, the streets hung with tapestry, fountains running wine ... I stood in the Strand, and beheld it, and blessed God,' wrote John Evelyn of Charles II's return to England on 29 May 1660.

'A bold and merry slut' – Nell Gwynne

Nell Gwynne rose from the gutter. She was born in a London alleyway, her father died in prison, and her alcoholic mother kept a brothel where young Nell served drinks. She worked briefly as an orange-seller in Drury Lane before becoming an actress at the Theatre Royal. Here Nell attracted King Charles' attention, and became his mistress at the age of 19. He remained her lover for the rest of his life. 'Let not poor Nelly starve,' Charles implored on his deathbed.

Sir Peter Lely's painting of Nell Gwynne hangs in the National Portrait Gallery in London. Having had two previous lovers named Charles, Nell mischievously renamed the monarch 'her Charles III'. Nell was to outlive the king by only a couple of years.

estoring the monarchy in 1660 put a smile back on the face of the nation following the dour years of the Commonwealth. Charles II reigned over a kingdom full of enterprise and creative endeavour that introduced banks and the Royal Mail, while the king's passion for science led to the establishment of the Royal Society and the Royal Observatory in Greenwich. Christopher Wren built St Paul's Cathedral, and the poet John Milton wrote *Paradise Lost.* Restoration comedy sparkled in newly reopened theatres, with women on the stage for the first time – including a teenage actress named Nell Gwynne. At home, the opposing political parties first became known as Whigs and Tories, and, abroad, New York was acquired from the Dutch.

Charles spent the first night of his reign in bed with his mistress, the beautiful yet temperamental Barbara Villiers, who bore him five children between 1661 and 1665, yet still found time to take as her lover John Churchill, who later became Duke of Marlborough. The king had a string of conspicuous mistresses, including Louise de Keroualle, dispatched to England by the wily French king specifically to become Charles' mistress and spy on him. But the most famous of them all was Nell Gwynne.

The Restoration Court was glamorous, opulent and extravagant, with the self-indulgent king surrounded by fashionably attired, second-rate advisors and voluptuous, provocatively pouting ladies. London took its cue from the Court, becoming a lively, fun-loving place, closely observed and recorded by Samuel Pepys in his diaries. Pepys could be highly critical of 'the sad, vicious and negligent Court, and all sober men fearful of the ruin of the whole kingdom.' Although mistrustful and cynical, Charles II was, however, also intelligent, witty and a shrewd politician.

The reign of the popular 'Merry Monarch' also witnessed disasters – the Great Plague of 1665 was quickly followed by the Great Fire of London, and a Dutch fleet sailed unopposed up the Thames, setting fire to English ships at anchor and towing away the king's flagship. However, it was Charles' lack of a legitimate heir that ultimately caused a major problem, since it led to his Roman Catholic brother, James, becoming king.

This earthenware cup with its image of Charles II, c.1660, has the appearance of a modern-day coronation mug. People in England drank tea and coffee for the first time during the Stuart era. Charles introduced yacht racing into England and popularised skating and horse racing.

Charles II dances with Mary of Orange at a ball at the Hague in Holland on the eve of the Restoration, giving a foretaste of the gaiety to come in the reign of the 'Merry Monarch'.

Plague and Fire

On a sweltering June day in 1665, Samuel Pepys was horrified to see houses in Drury Lane with large red crosses painted on their doors. Bubonic plague had returned to London, a dreaded disease caught when bitten by fleas carried by rats, which thrived in the appallingly filthy city. Dark red blotches all over the body led to high fever, delirium and an agonising death. There was no known cure.

The death toll mounted rapidly. By August it had reached 1,000 a day and hundreds of bodies were heaped into huge pits. Many people fled the city. Daniel Defoe's *Journal of the Plague Year* graphically describes a deserted city where all normal life has ceased. Dense black smoke billowed from huge bonfires, lit in an attempt to purify the air. Corpses littered empty streets. By the time the winter cold ended this calamity it was estimated that over 100,000 people had died.

A second catastrophe occurred the following year. The Great Fire of London began during the early hours of Sunday morning, on 2 September, at a bakery in Pudding Lane in the heart of the City. The courtyard of the Star Inn next door was full of straw, and tons of highly inflammable goods lay in warehouses in nearby

This picture of Samuel Pepys was painted by John Hayles in 1666. Pepys had begun his diary six years earlier when the monarchy was restored. His original manuscript is in the library at Magdalene College, his old university college in Cambridge.

Doctors who attended victims of the plague tried to protect themselves from infection. Many wore a bizarre, beak-shaped mask filled with herbs, in the hope that the herbs would protect them from the disease.

Thames Street. Flames spread rapidly through closely packed timber houses, fanned by a strong breeze. There being no hoses or fire brigades, the resulting inferno quickly raged out of control. Roman Catholics or foreigners were blamed for causing it.

The Great Fire burned for four days and nights, only ceasing when the wind changed direction and the flames blew back over already devastated ground. By then the City, including St Paul's Cathedral, was a smouldering ruin. More than 13,000 houses had been destroyed, and 100,000 people made homeless. Miraculously no one was killed and a new City of London was soon to rise from the smoking ruins. Brick and stone replaced the timber construction of the old medieval city, reducing the risk of fire and providing fewer opportunities for rats to breed — it was the last outbreak of bubonic plague in London.

This plague bell, now displayed in the Museum of London, was rung by those collecting corpses in handcarts by night, while uttering the mournful cry, 'Bring out your dead.'

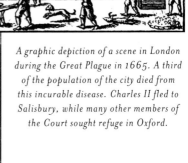

A graphic depiction of a scene in London during the Great Plague in 1665. A third of the population of the city died from this incurable disease. Charles II fled to Salisbury, while many other members of the Court sought refuge in Oxford.

Lieve Verschuier's portrayal of the Great Fire. The old St Paul's Cathedral is ablaze and flames approach London Bridge and the Tower of London, as terrified citizens seek the safety of the River Thames.

The Glorious Revolution

Sir Peter Lely's portrait of James II with his first wife, Anne Hyde, Protestant mother of both Mary and Anne. She was the daughter of the Earl of Clarendon, one of the more capable politicians in the second half of the 17th century.

James II's reign was one of the shortest in English history. Nicknamed 'Dismal Jimmy' by Nell Gwynne and barely three years on the throne, his offensively autocratic attitude — 'know I am King, I will be obeyed' — alienated the Church, Parliament, the army, and even his own daughters, Anne and Mary, wife of William of Orange, leader of the Dutch Republic.

James had converted to Catholicism and unwisely championed a faith deeply unpopular in England. In 1688, the birth of a son threatened the Protestant succession. William of Orange was invited by a group of peers to replace James and rule jointly with Mary, an equally devout Protestant.

William and Mary are presented with the crown of England — but it came with strings attached. The Declaration of Rights set stringent limits on royal power — no monarch could henceforth override the laws of Parliament, be a Roman Catholic or marry into that faith.

The east wind bringing William's fleet from Holland kept the English ships trapped in the Thames. William landed in South Devon unopposed by James II. Fearing a similar fate to his father, 'Dismal Jimmy' fled to France. He attempted a comeback two years later by invading Ireland, but was soundly defeated at the Battle of the Boyne, an event still celebrated by Irish Protestants. James spent the rest of his life in exile.

On 21 June 1694 the Bank of England first opened its door in Lincoln's Inn Fields in London, amidst howls of protest from long established, privately owned banks such as Hoares, which, like the Bank of England, still exists today.

William was a consummate statesman and a shrewd judge of character, yet suffered poor health and lacked social graces — he was dismissed by the fastidious ladies of the Court as 'a low Dutch bear'. His main reason for accepting the English crown was to secure a powerful ally for his relentless conflict with the French, and soon involved England in a long and costly continental war. The Bank of England was formed in 1694 to help finance it.

William III established a harmonious relationship with Parliament, where Whigs and Tories were in continuous struggle for political supremacy. Mary was a popular queen but died of smallpox aged only 33, after barely six years on the throne. William reigned a further eight years before dying after falling from his horse in the grounds of Hampton Court. William's sister-in-law, Anne, became queen in 1702, the 1701 Act of Succession having ensured Protestant continuity. During William's reign his people enjoyed a prosperous and mainly peaceful existence. When the European war finally ended in 1713, the nation had become the world's major power for the first time in its history.

A contemporary playing card portrays the beheading of the Duke of Monmouth in the Tower of London, after his abortive rebellion against James II. Three years later, James had become massively unpopular and William of Orange acquired the throne without further bloodshed.

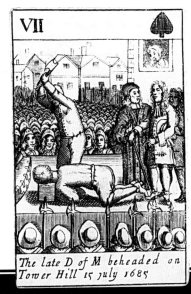

The Monmouth Rebellion

In 1685 the Duke of Monmouth, illegitimate son of Charles II, mounted a coup to seize the kingdom. His army, however, was slaughtered by James II's crack troops at Sedgemoor in Somerset, the last ever battle fought on English soil. Survivors were tried by the notorious Bloody Judge Jeffreys, then hanged or sent as forced labour to the sugar plantations in Barbados. Monmouth was executed as a traitor; only a few escaped, including the writer Daniel Defoe.

Art Fit for a King

The Stuarts were enthusiastic patrons of the arts. King James I commissioned Inigo Jones to create the elegant Queen's House at Greenwich and the Banqueting House at Whitehall Palace. Jones made his name as a theatrical set designer and, having visited Italy, introduced Palladianism – a neoclassical style of architecture – into England. He also created the piazza at Covent Garden and the glorious Single and Double Cube Rooms at Wilton House near Salisbury, ancestral home of the earls of Pembroke.

Flemish-born Anthony Van Dyck was appointed by Charles I as his Court Painter and he produced a series of superb portraits of the king. Examples of his work can be seen in Wilton House, the 4th Earl of Pembroke

Inigo Jones' superb Double Cube Room in Wilton House near Salisbury. The painting at the end of the room is the largest ever painted by Van Dyck. The room was originally used as a dining room for state visits, but in more recent times it has featured in films such as The Madness of King George *and* Sense and Sensibility.

being Charles' Lord Chamberlain. Van Dyck considerably influenced subsequent English portrait painters. Charles also engaged Rubens to paint the ceiling at the Banqueting House, where a few years later the king was to step out of a first-floor window onto a scaffold to be executed. Subsequently Cromwell sold the king's art collection to help pay for the Civil War.

Another Flemish artist, Peter Lely, was employed by Charles II as his Court Painter and he painted numerous portraits of the king, his many mistresses, and other ladies of the Court. Lely became so popular that he established a 'portrait factory', where an army of assistants churned out pictures for him to sign. Charles also commissioned Anthony Verrio to paint friezes and ceilings at Windsor. Verrio worked at places such as Chatsworth and Burghley, where his dramatic Heaven and Hell Rooms are located. Grinling Gibbons began working in Charles' reign, and his exquisite wood carvings can be seen today at St Paul's Cathedral, the Royal Hospital Chelsea and Petworth House in Sussex. The king's most inspired move was to appoint Christopher Wren as his Surveyor General.

William and Mary disliked the sprawling, unhealthy medieval palace at Whitehall, so commissioned Wren to create Kensington Palace and radically extend the old Tudor palace at Hampton Court. The talented amateur, Vanbrugh, was chosen instead of Wren, however, to create Blenheim Palace during Anne's reign – an outstanding period of English domestic architecture.

A copy of Van Dyck's Self Portrait with a Sunflower *hangs in Ham House, Surrey. Ham House was built in 1610 and is one of the nation's outstanding Stuart houses, with fine examples of work by Verrio and seascapes by Van der Velde.*

Roger Pratt created Kingston Lacy in Dorset for the Bankes' family after their original home at nearby Corfe Castle was destroyed during the Civil War. The keys of the castle are now in the library of the house, which retains its archetypal Restoration façade.

An exquisite example of Grinling Gibbon's wood carving at Hampton Court Palace. Gibbons also created the bronze statue of Charles II which stands in the courtyard of the Royal Hospital Chelsea, founded by the king.

Sir Christopher Wren

Johann Closterman's portrait of Christopher Wren as President of The Royal Society c.1683. Wren's great masterpiece, St Paul's Cathedral, is shown in the background. It was the first domed building in England.

Christopher Wren, England's best-known architect and creator of some of the nation's most beautiful buildings, had no formal architectural training, designing nothing before he was 30. Sixth child of a Wiltshire parson, Wren was a brilliant scientist and mathematician, and was Professor of Astronomy at Oxford University at the time of his first commissions – Oxford's Sheldonian Theatre and a new chapel for Pembroke College, Cambridge.

King Charles II appointed Wren as his Surveyor General in 1669. The Great Fire had provided a unique architectural opportunity to completely rebuild the devastated City of London. A week after the fire, Wren presented a breathtakingly bold and imaginative plan of sweeping avenues, great piazzas and noble vistas. Sadly this visionary concept was considered too radical and firmly rejected, yet out of the ashes rose 52 churches designed by Wren, including St Brides and St Mary-le-Bow, together with his finest achievement – St Paul's Cathedral.

Canaletto's glorious panoramic picture Greenwich Hospital from the north bank of the Thames depicts Wren's elegant design for the naval equivalent of the Royal Hospital Chelsea, with Inigo Jones' tiny Queen's House in the background.

The Fountain Court at Hampton Court Palace links the old Tudor buildings with Wren's magnificent extension, built for William and Mary towards the end of the 17th century. The pedimented first-floor windows, carved stone circles and square windows above are considered by some critics to be over fussy.

Although unhindered by today's planning procedures and building regulations, Wren was invariably constrained by his patrons' conservatism and financial resources, which lacked the seemingly bottomless purse of the Vatican or Louis XIV of France, the Sun King. Wren was always conscious that good architecture was not an artistic ego-trip, but the creation of buildings that are pleasing to the eye and successfully fulfil a functional purpose. The majority of Wren's buildings, such as the Royal Hospital Chelsea and his library at Trinity College, Cambridge, are still used for their original purposes. They continue to be admired three centuries later, their timeless appeal enhanced by exquisite settings, still mostly unspoilt. By the time he died at the age of 91, Wren, the scientist with an artist's eye, had inspired a classic period of English architecture which, through Vanbrugh, Gibbs, Adam, Wood and Nash, was to last over 200 years.

Emmanuel College Chapel in Cambridge was built between 1668 and 1673. The high pedimented centre echoes classical temples and the jaunty cupola is typically Wren.

The Sheldonian Theatre at Oxford University was endowed by Bishop Gilbert Sheldon, formerly warden of All Soul's College. The first university ceremony was held here in 1669 and today it is still used for formal ceremonial occasions.

A Literary Age

England's reputation as a literary nation, established during Elizabeth's reign, continued during the Stuart era. William Shakespeare wrote his great tragedies, *King Lear, Anthony and Cleopatra, Othello* and *Macbeth* in the reign of James I. Performances of *King Lear*, Shakespeare's tale of a king rejected by unscrupulous daughters, were banned while Mary and Anne were on the throne.

John Donne's poetry is characterised by subtle imagery and delicate rhythm. His best-known verse is probably 'Go and catch a falling star', while his love poems are full of tenderness and passion.

Masques — plays with music, colourful costumes and scenery — were exceedingly popular with Stuart courtiers, who adored dressing up. Ben Jonson wrote many of the plays, while Inigo Jones designed the costumes and scenery.

Unlike Shakespeare, none of John Donne's verse was published in his lifetime, yet he is now widely regarded as an outstanding English poet. A former Roman Catholic, Donne became Dean of St Paul's in 1621 and was noted for his eloquent sermons.

John Bunyan was conscripted into the Parliamentary army at the age of 16. Arrested for seditious preaching, he wrote his best-known work, *The Pilgrim's Progress*, while in prison. John Milton created *Paradise Lost* after he had gone completely blind, apparently conceiving it while he was asleep.

'Bunyan's Dream' is the title of the frontispiece to the 4th edition of The Pilgrim's Progress, *published in 1680. Much of the great literature of the Stuart age is religious in nature. The most enduring masterpiece is the King James' Bible, produced by a group of academics and published in 1611.*

The title page of the 1645 edition of Milton's Miscellaneous Poems. *After he went blind, Milton's verses were written down rather begrudgingly by his daughters, who did not share their father's passion for poetry.*

POEMS
OF
Mr. *John Milton*,
BOTH
ENGLISH and LATIN,
Compos'd at several times.

Printed by his true Copies.

The S o n g s were set in Musick by Mr. H E N R Y L A W E S Gentleman of the K I N G S Chappel, and one of His M A I E S T I E S Private Musick.

— *Baccare frontem*
Cingite, ne vati noceat mala lingua futuro,
Virgil, Eclog. 7.

Printed and publish'd according to
ORDER.

LONDON,
Printed by *Ruth Raworth* for *Humphrey Moseley*, and are to be sold at the signe of the Princes Arms in S. *Pauls* Church-yard. 1645.

Drama flourished after Charles II was restored to the throne. John Dryden's satirical verse and sophisticated comedy made him as popular a playwright in his day as Shakespeare had once been, whilst the former barrister, William Congreve, later became the leading writer of Restoration comedy.

The diaries of Samuel Pepys and John Evelyn vividly describe the England of Charles II. Pepys witnessed some of the most dramatic events of the Stuart age – the execution of Charles I, the Restoration of the monarchy and coronation of Charles II, the Plague and the Great Fire of London. Pepys wrote more than one million words before being forced to give up, as he too was going blind. Daniel Defoe's childhood memories of the Plague led to his *Journal of the Plague Year*. He went on to write *Moll Flanders* and *Robinson Crusoe*, and is regarded by many critics as the nation's first great novelist, although Aphra Behn had published *Oroonoko*, a novel and romance about slavery set in Surinam, in 1688.

Satire achieved new heights through Alexander Pope and Jonathan Swift, accurately reflecting the witty cynicism of the age – cool, clever and cultivated. Pope coined memorable phrases, such as 'a little knowledge is a dangerous thing' and 'fools rush in where angels fear to tread'. Dublin-born Swift's best-known work is *Gulliver's Travels*. Newspapers became popular and periodicals, such as Richard Steele's *Spectator* and *Tatler*, first appeared.

The Passionate Poet – John Milton

When a student at Christ's College, Cambridge, Milton was known as 'the Lady of Christ's', on account of his fine features. A devoted propagandist for the Puritan cause and passionate supporter of Cromwell, Milton was fortunate to escape retribution after the Restoration. However Charles II was a tolerant man and allowed the publication of Milton's finest works, *Paradise Lost, Paradise Regained* and *Samson Agonistes*.

The frontispiece of The Sceptical Chemist *by Robert Boyle (1627–91), the eminent physicist and chemist. Boyle was one of the pioneers of rational scientific thought and helped to instigate an age of innovation.*

The Age of Reason Begins

During the 17th century, science emerged from the shadowy world of alchemy and sorcery. John Dee, that venerable Elizabethan alchemist, had died in the early years of James I's reign. Dee claimed that he could turn base metal into gold, yet ended his days a pauper. In 1605, Francis Bacon's seminal work *The Advancement of Learning* established the beginning of rational scientific method. The brilliant yet mercurial Bacon died in 1626, having caught a fatal chill conducting a rather bizarre experiment involving chickens immersed in ice. In 1628, William Harvey discovered that the heart pumped blood around the body. This discovery totally contradicted the accepted view at the time and Harvey's theory was at first much mocked, although it was accepted in his own lifetime.

During the reign of Charles II, Isaac Newton, one of the greatest scientists of all time, discovered the laws of gravity, proved that all colours are contained in white light, and invented calculus. He did not publish his findings straight away. Architect Christopher Wren was also a prominent mathematician and astronomer at Oxford. One day Wren and Edmond Halley, who first saw the comet named after him, were wondering what forces moved the planets. Halley went to Cambridge to ask Newton. When Newton revealed his theory of gravity complete with proof, Halley was amazed and persuaded Newton to publish it. Halley even arranged and paid for the printing himself.

The Irish scientist Robert Boyle is regarded as the father of modern physics and chemistry. He formulated atomic theory, and discovered the laws of gases known as Boyle's Law, still learned by science students today. As the

Sir Isaac Newton's rooms were located in the Great Court at Trinity College, Cambridge, between the chapel and the Great Gate. Here he conceived his Principia, *arguably the most important scientific work ever published. Newton resided at Trinity for 35 years having entered the college in 1661, the year after the Restoration.*

17th century progressed, advances in technology produced logarithms, slide rules, microscopes, forceps and air-pumps. Robert Hooke invented the compound microscope and wheel barometer. At the same time experiments with vivisection and blood transfusion were undertaken.

John Locke and Thomas Hobbes were the foremost philosophers of the time, Locke's radical concepts influencing political theory for generations to come. In 1660, Wren, Boyle and other immensely talented men founded the Royal Society. Their enlightened work meant that logic and reason replaced mumbo-jumbo, providing a firm platform for scientific advancement, fully researched, tested and evaluated.

A contemporary detailed sketch of a louse, as observed through the newly invented microscope.

This Victorian painting by Robert Hannah depicts the physician William Harvey demonstrating his theory of the circulation of the blood to Charles I. The king was a keen amateur scientist.

A Supreme Scientist — Sir Isaac Newton

Newton became a student at Trinity College, Cambridge, in 1661 and was elected a Fellow at the age of 26. By then he had made his great discoveries in astronomy, optics and mathematics. He left Cambridge in 1696 to become Master of the Royal Mint. President of the Royal Society in 1703 and knighted in 1705, Newton died aged 85 and is buried in Westminster Abbey.

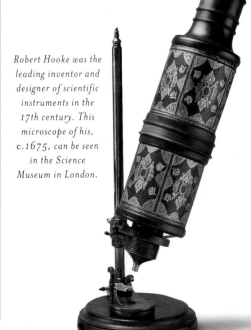

Robert Hooke was the leading inventor and designer of scientific instruments in the 17th century. This microscope of his, c.1675, can be seen in the Science Museum in London.

The End of an Era

Queen Anne was unprepared for monarchy, yet, while happiest drinking tea and playing cards far into the night, proved to be a conscientious and capable monarch. She was very stout, in constant pain from gout and, although she conceived 17 children, none of them outlived her.

This 18th-century painting shows the 1st Duke of Marlborough on horseback signing the famous dispatch to his wife, Sarah, announcing his glorious victory over Louis XIV's army at Blenheim in 1704.

Sir Godfrey Kneller's portrait of Queen Anne shows her in her robes of state. She ruled England for 12 years, leaving the kingdom a supremely powerful and prosperous nation, respected throughout the world.

Sarah, Duchess of Marlborough, playing a popular 17th-century card game called 'Pope Joan' with Lady Fitzharding (shown on the left), one of Queen Anne's ladies-in-waiting and reputedly once mistress of William of Orange.

Queen Anne in the House of Lords surrounded by scarlet-clad peers and befrocked bishops. The most important legislation enacted by Parliament during her lifetime was the Act of Succession in 1701 and the Act of Union in 1707.